AF434074

contents

You call it "Love"

…

Beautiful Girl

—

Stolen glances.
Secret notes.
Distortion of reality occurs.

He can no longer control himself.
The sight of her awakens tender feelings -
That were once buried deep down
From the last time he got his heart broken.

He prays that this time it will be different...

An increase in hope, a decrease in fear.
Her smooth lips against his cheeks.
The way her hips sway as she walks his way.

How can he stop thinking of that lovely soul?
How could he not wish, not want more?

Beautiful Girl.
The glory in her eyes
Overwhelms him inside.
Beautiful Girl.
That precious smile -
She is all that he desires.

If only she was truly his...

You Can Live Inside Of Me

—

I will get stronger
So my heart can carry all of you inside of me
And never let you go

Remedy

—

A tempting desire arises when
I look inside your eyes.
Such history and mystery,
concealed by just one smile.

To rob me of my conscious and
free me of distress,
Makes you the best of demons
that I have ever met.

Now take me away, down the
empty hidden hole,
And promise me to cure all of
my broken soul...

Cigarette

—

Turning towards you,
Being wrapped inside your arms,
I feel the warmth of your breath on my forehead,
The comforts of you on my skin.

Breathing in every part of you.
Breathing out every part of me.

I get lost in your eyes even when you look away.
I get hypnotized by your smile even when you glare at me.

Your anger excites me, your joy amuses me.
Nothing truly matters when you are away from me.

Breathing in every part of you.
Breathing out every part of me.

...

...

Paranoid without you,
Turning selfish when in desperate need of you.

My carelessness caused me to become addicted.
This lust for you keeps growing like a monster in me.

Breathing in every part of you.
Breathing out every part of me.

Oh baby, you can hurt me all you want.
You must know that I will still be here.
Just long enough before my need for you slowly kills me.

These deadly toxins are burning my insides,
But nothing will stop me from whispering
"I love you".

Breathing for You

Your lips are filled with poison
But all I want to do
Is kiss them

suffocating

if i asked you to let me breathe,
would you move your hands away from my neck?

Forest of Love

—

'Forget him!'
These words are ringing in my mind
My skin still burns from the places where his hands were
The blue, the purple, and the red,
A rainbow painted on my body

'Forget him!'
Oh! I couldn't agree more!
And yet I long for his presence, desire his acceptance
I pray to God for his return
My savior, my angel

...

...

'Forget him!'
I am drowning, suffocating, and yet I need more rain
The freezing drops are soft kisses against my cheeks
The kisses that you promised me
The kisses that were stolen by Time

'Forget him!'
I am on my knees. Crawling,
Through the garden of roses you named after me
My thighs are bleeding and yet the thorns feel pleasant,
They feel like home
They feel like you

'Forget him!'
But I cannot...
Because the cuts and tears and broken bones
Will not stop the warmth of sunshine that I feel
When I am wrapped in his Loving arms.

Sacred Lotus

—

The scent of innocence clung onto her,
Spreading over to those passing by,
Cleansing them of their sins.

The purity of her soul overwhelmed those in the wrong,
They knew they stood no chance against her goodness.
Her ability to start over, to let go of the past,
Was mesmerizing to those that have fallen.

She became an inspiration
A motivation
To all who were around

Praise to her, the creation of the Sun.
The joy, the light,
That she shone upon them, made them all feel worthy.

The love for her grew stronger,
Spread quicker,
Until she was not enough to sustain the desires of others.
And so they took her.
Not willing to share.
They ruined her.

They put an end to the Lotus.

Intoxicated Love

—

My mind is intoxicated with your lies.
I need you to save me, make me feel alive…

You call it 'Love'

—

Red imprints of your hands are left
on my neck
Purple kisses of your fists are left
on my thighs

~

I lose my breath when we cuddle
My fingers go numb when we hold hands

~

As you decorate my body with your
glance
I begin to find beauty in the unique
designs of your creation

The Price of You and Me

—

Together we stood looking out into the sunset,
The perfect mixture of purple, pink, and orange.
A sunset that seemed to last forever.

And that's what we had hoped for. The never ending sunset,
So we could cherish every second by each other's side.

Lips locked and hands held tight we waited for the sun to disappear.
And when it finally vanished into the emptiness that surrounded us,
It did not feel too bad. Not bad at all.

But all I had to do was look up,
To realize that you were no longer by my side.
You disappeared with the sun; with the purple, pink, and orange.

I remained frozen. Absorbed by nothingness.
The love we shared was purifying and yet it was too good to last.
And although I want you back...
There was a price to pay for our happiness.
For joy and pleasure, whose deadline we thought we could surpass.
And so we had to pay for it all...

The Price of You and Me.

A Single Mutation
Can Ruin The World

—

I'd like to think that I can speak to you

with my mind. That our thoughts are

interlinked, intertwined,

like our DNA which can only be altered by a mutation.

What is the mutation of our relationship?

Is it the force? Is it the fear? Is it the lack of trust?

is it me?

is it me?

is it me?

Till Desth Do Us Part

You've sewn your heart on mine
With a needle the size of a knife

Butterfly Effect

—

At 5 years old
She liked a boy
That told her she was "pretty".
They sat hand in hand
And played pretend
That they were "Oh so ready!"
She told her friends
And they all giggled without an end.

At 10 years old
She liked a boy
That told her she was "gross".
"Too much hair! Look at that fat!
I'd rather like a monkey instead!"
Tears rolled down,
Self-esteem broke.
She told no one,
Because she already knew
What she was...

At 15 years old
She liked a boy
That told her she was "beautiful".
So strong and tall,
She gave no thought
But loved him always more.
"He is no good for you"
"Find someone better"
She let these words fly past.
They stood hand in hand
Against the world
They always stood together.

...

...

But something changed...

No longer interested in her
"I cannot wait any more!"
He robbed her of her flower once,
And then once more.
Regret and tears,
Nothing more.
She held it all inside too long.
She asked for help.
In need of aid.
But got nothing more
Than blue, purple, and red,
All over her.

At 17 years old
She liked no one.
She went nowhere.
She did nothing.
She wanted forgiveness.
She wanted life to simply end.
No words to speak.
Only thoughts filled her now.
The "Why?" and "What?" and "How?"
They almost killed her.
She cried all night,
She sat all day,
With nothing else getting in her way.
All alone,
No longer her,
Thinking of the best way
To finally give in
And say

Goodbye...

Longing

...

Protected by the Sun

—

I close my eyes and try to think of something nice
Something that has made me smile
Something that has made me laugh

And I think about the days that weren't all that tough

When the sun rays danced lightly on my skin
When the wind whispered softly in my ears

When you sat by my side
Holding my body close to yours
Protecting me with your strong arms
Feeling the beating of my heart in your chest

The Other Woman

—

The realization dawns upon me.
I was destined to be
the other woman.

The woman
that all men want, but no one wants to be with.

The woman
that has short-term happiness, but will never feel fulfilled.
I will be her my whole life.

One day I might even accept it.

Fake Love

I still remember the day you took my hand,
Kissed my forehead,
And told me you didn't love me.

Ghosts of Lovers

—

The Ghosts of fallen Lovers,
Wandering the World.
Aimlessly waiting for a Spark,
And a little bit of Hope.
Sadness overgrown them,
Spreading like a wildfire,
Now became contagious.
A disease.

The Ghosts of fallen Lovers,
Broken by the Truth.
Questioning reality,
Slowly losing their morality.
Desperate for belonging, but -
Desired by none.
The World now dark,
No light, no brightness.

The Ghosts of fallen Lovers,
They got what they deserved.
But now revenge is coming,
Prepare for what is worse.

Hercules

—

He was my forever rose.
The beauty that he possessed was irresistible,
To the point where the pain of his thorns began to feel pleasant.
Joy.

He was my elixir.
Designed to blind me from everything but love for him.
And so I left my life to join his, in hopes of living in this eternal lie.
Obsession.

He was Hercules.
The hero of my imagination. A hero of my own making.
Designed to have pride, power, loyalty, trust... All you could wish for.
Naivety.

He was my work of art.
A collage of his best traits, that I put together myself.
Only to have each piece go through self-destruction. It wouldn't last.
Disappointment.

He was the abuser.
Using my weaknesses against me.
Through words and actions, he tore through the petals of the Lotus.
The End.

You proved to be manipulative.
I proved to be a fool.

By the Lonely River

—

By the lonely river

I sat waiting for you
Hoping that you would come back for me.
We would hold hands and talk about the future we never received,
Laugh about the endless memories that were never made,
But you were just like the long, cold river,
And I knew you would not stop for me.
So I sat aimlessly, alone,

By the lonely river.

i lost a piece of me in you
that i try to find in every boy i meet
reading them like books
i give the boring ones away
hoping to exchange them for something
that will bring me back to you

praying for wholeness

Water For The Soul

—

In a room full of people, I meet your gaze and wonder:
Do they all feel the tension rise in the room?
Can they smell the fire burning inside me?
Will they silence the voices murmuring in my head?

No one notices.
No one knows.

Intensity is a form of distraction you use to send my mind
into microgravity where you can snatch my clarity
away from me and pull me towards you like a magnet
as you have become the center of gravity but
my thoughts have already vanished into outer space
and the only thing I have left is my feelings that push me
towards You

They notice.
They know.

...

...

Judgment is a subjective way of knowing,
but they know, when they see your clear blue eyes,
your sharp jaw, your muscular frame.
They see what they want to see, they always have.
And I can't judge them.
Hypocrisy is the enemy of Truth, and I too have once saw
God in You

You see me, stripped of my armor.
I see You, but my tears make you so blurry...

For years,
I tried my best to forget you,
To replace you,
With food, With exercise,
And if there was a patch, I swear to God
I would wear it. But right now,
I want to forget about the pain.
Because I miss You.

I would give up air to kiss you once more

—

Heat infused the atmosphere with the rapid movement

of our bodies.

Kinetic energy that we created

melted glaciers and moved mountains.

Inextricable even by saw, Our lips were constantly interlocked

tightly,

Breathing each other in, because

air became entirely negligible

to us.

hotel by the side of the road

—

she said she saw you in that hotel
and now I quietly beg her to take me there
never wanting to miss the opportunity of accidentally
seeing you myself.
we drive by the hotel often and I can see you
with my eyes closed,
sitting inside the lobby I have never been in,
imagining you eating in a restaurant that only exists in my mind.
perhaps,
that's it,
you are just in my mind

Crawling back to you

—

I said I would not write about you
But here I am, once more.

It's all because I banned you from my heart
Yet you managed to stay in my mind
Crawling back every night
To steal my reasoning away from me
Leaving me blind
Making me follow my emotions
Until I reach you, once more.

Dreams

At last, we meet again.

So deeply devoted to one another,
Our hearts beat to the same rhythm.
"Boom. Boom."

That charming gaze, delightful smile.
I let you carry me away.

And off we go.
Flying through the cotton clouds,
Eyes filled with happy tears,
Never wanting it to end.

"Destiny awaits us!"
So utterly consumed in each other.
Two love birds unable to let go.

The softness of your palm against my cheek,
Leaning in too close,
Laughing at our little jokes.

Everything is finally falling into the proper place.

But at last,
I wake up.

And you are gone once more.

late night thoughts

sometimes I wonder what I would do if I were to see you again
would I run the opposite direction, or right into your arms?

There is sunshine on my cheek but I can't feel the warmth.

—

Three years have passed, and yet I'm still
trapped
inside your big, loving, suffocating arms.
And I still can't decide if I want you to let go,
or hold tighter.
Truth is, I can breathe all the same. I just
don't know if the air
satisfies me anymore.

CHV

Your hand moving up my thigh,
Your lips on my neck,
Our bodies intertwined.

Things might have ended roughly, but every fortnight
I think about you
Dreaming of what could have been
Wishing that we still had a choice, an option, a chance..

If I could do it all over again, I would.
I would cry and scream and fight, but in the end of it all
I would have spent another year with you.
Kissing, Hugging,
Making memories
with You

Why can't it all be simple?

See the truth is, I love you.
But loving you causes too much pain,
so I must learn
to love myself instead.

Gone

...

Once again, I dreamt of you.
You came to visit me and
we lived
as if nothing had happened. But I woke up
sadder than usual, realizing we would never relive
these memories. How I wish that I could sleep
forever. To never wake up
in a world that you are no longer a part of.
Let me live
in my dreams
with you.

Endless Cycle of Nothing

—

Everything was falling apart.

Life was being crushed by all these Hopes and Dreams
That one has created for themselves but could never reach.
No matter the effort, Nothing worked out.
It was an endless cycle of disappointment...

You were there too. You stood and watched.
And yet were blind to all that was happening.
You did not feel that fire,
You did not feel the pain,
You ignored the tsunami of issues that consumed me whole.

How could you?
How could you be so oblivious to the torture I was put through?
Why did you?
Why did you leave when I needed you most?

Death is a joke and I can't stop laughing...

Pain

The worst thing about Pain is that it is inevitable.
As humans, we never know when it will strike us.
We can only wait and hope for the best.

But with Pain, comes its best friend Anxiety,
And when those two come together,
They become a killer team.

Tell me I did not warn you,
Of the harm that was to come
The grief that overtook your soul…
And now you are gone.

Dance of Death

—

And seeing them together
~Their eyes filled with affection~
Felt like being stabbed in the chest with a dull knife.

Pain spreading through my body like a disease,
Infected with the sorrow of rejection and replacement,
Torturing me day and night without an end.

So awful it is, to finally realize that you were never 'The One',
That there was always 'The Other'.
To realize that your Hope has vanished into thin air,
That Faith has been murdered by their lies.

Desire to disappear has never been so strong.
Lulling me further and further away.
I allow my destiny to be controlled by my shattered heart.

I would like to let you go, but my mind is filled with
thoughts of you. If I go a day without thinking of you,
you appear in my dreams.

There is simply no escaping you.

You have full control over my life, and I proceed to live with you in
my memories, my hopes, my dreams.
Or perhaps they are nightmares? For I don't truly want to see you.

And so I ask, I beg, I pray
that You let me go instead.

"If you love them, let them go",
but what if I don't?

Realm Of Fallen Souls

—

Did it mean nothing to you?
When I opened up the gates to the complex realm
Filled with broken, burning particles of stars
That never got their opportunity to shine.
It was open just for you. Just for those few seconds.
You did not come in. You did not leave either.
How ignorant of you to keep those gates open.
To dismiss those pieces as if they were dust,
Leaving me more empty handed and broken than before.

You are gone.
But you will never feel that pain, that emptiness -
The only feelings that are left in me.
As I slowly fade away into the dark deep realm of a greater creation.

The realm of fallen souls.

Imprint

Standing in the shower, I try to scrub the sense of you away.
I try so hard, with such force and effort,
that my skin starts to peel off.
It's turning red

And yet you are still here.
Your lips pressed against mine, your skin burning into me.
And I'm taken back, to those awful days,
When I said no, and you pretended not to hear.

13/03/17

You took my most precious gem away from me,
And left me empty handed.

You shattered my soul into billions of pieces,
And left me broken on the streets.

Your selfishness destroyed me,
And caused the remainder of hope to vanish into thin air.

I am decaying...

My only question is,
Why didn't you kill me instead?

Followed By Blue Eyes

—

Did I see you?
Was it you walking behind me today?
Or have I gone completely insane?

I'm painting your face on strangers
Seeing you in the eyes of other men
Visioning you like a ghost in a haunted house.

I let your presence surround me
Invade me.
And yet it isn't even you, just a dream, just an illusion

Oblivious

—

Oblivious to the reality I live in,
I'm slowly driven insane by the madness surrounding me.
The walls that have been build up from stories you told me,
Are now shattered with lies.
They break above me, suffocating me with their heaviness.
And yet it feels like nothing worse than my day-to-day life.
Maybe I'm used to it? Or maybe you just ruined me this much…

I see you with my eyes closed. Why can't you disappear?

How long until I stop writing about you? Seeing you in my dreams?
Another year? Another month? Another day?
Or perhaps this is the last time.
That's a lie.
Even in death, you would be on my mind,
Lurking.
My biggest regret, and my biggest achievement.

Life became unpredictable
Too hard to handle, Too difficult to follow
A cry for help would result in the loss of time
And yet remaining silent would almost eat me alive

Death became wanted
Constantly desired, Constantly thought of
No one knew, but me and my best friend scissors
There was nothing here that could make me want to stay

And that is when I
Became an

Accidental Poet.

Eight days too Late

—

When you left, I made a decision to get rid of
everything you gave me,
everything you touched,
everything you looked at,
everything you liked.
I burned the poems and tore the pictures and chopped off all my hair
But the essence of you was still surrounding me
I searched for your presence in all the objects I owned but realized
too late
that you have merged our souls
with all the jokes, and all the memories, and all the unspoken words

When you left, you left a part of you behind.
You left a part of you in me.
So I cut my wrists, and my thighs, and my stomach.
And I cut more and I cut deeper.
Hoping that one of these many cuts will kill you before they get to
Me

Art that only a sick mind would appreciate

—

I want to cut out the fat from my thighs,
Carve my body into the sculpture that would make Michelangelo
jealous of my skills

Except that it wouldn't.
Because most don't find skeletons appealing to the eye

I promised him I would stop cutting, and I did

Basic Instinct

Because what I hated most was inside

And he was hurting it just fine without my help

Death is my Lover

—

Why are they afraid of you my love?
Can't they see you're perfect?

Taking me away on rides,
Trips, and on vacation.
You protect me from all of this,
Free me of these duties.
Make me feel like I am whole,
Surround me with all your beauties.

They all complain that you're no good,
But you're my only blessing.

I don't need another lover,
Darkness is the one I need,
He'll be gentle, not judgmental,
He's the only one I need.

I've always been his number one,
His favorite little girl,
He loved me since the start -
Day one!
I am his truly.

...

...

They can say what they want,
I am not afraid.
I love you,
And I promise to find a way
to stay with you
Regardless of my duties.

Oh Lover,
I can't wait until we are together.
I have a plan! I'll speed it up!
I'll be there soon, Oh Lover!

I found a tiny little tool,
That will bring us closer.
All I have to do is cut and see the substance
Red like love.

I'm ready,
I'll soon be gone.
No one stops me,
They've let me go.
And now I'm free,
And now I'm yours.

Oh Lover,
Take me in your arms,
And never let me go.
I am Yours,
And You are Mine.
Oh Lover, Oh Lover!

The Li(f)e You Live

You can't escape reality
When it hugs you like a casket
Ready to bury you deep into the ground

Dear Death,

Tomorrow morning, the sun will rise again,
And the moon will disappear.

I know I don't ask for much,
But I am in need of a favor.

Make it stop.
Please make it stop.

I don't want the sun or the moon.
I just want to be left alone, in the Dark.

I want it to stop.
The world to stop this cycle of madness.

But no one is listening to me,
And so I ask you.

My dear, lovely friend, Death,
End my misery, and end my pain.
Help me get out of this miserable game.

Shattered Soul

—

Do you see those shattered bricks on the ground?
The ones you kick every time you pass by?
That broken mess that you joke about with your friends?

That was my safe place.
Those dirty bricks were once much more.
They made up the walls around my heart.
A sanctuary.
Beautiful and gold.
They kept me safe from the harm that you bestowed upon me.
Thunder, storm, hurricane,
Nothing was capable of breaking it down.
It saved me from fire and from ice.
It helped me live, survive.

It could not be broken from the outside.
But you knew a way in.
You fooled that shy little girl into believing that you were the one.
Her naïve nature let you inside, with hopes
That you would bring flowers into that lonely sanctuary,
And fill it with Love.

You desired none of that.
You pulled her into the darkness
Where no moon and stars could reach her.
She was alone with a monster that she let inside herself.
And there, the deed was done.
Before she knew it, you were gone.
Leaving her empty and even more alone.

The walls fell slowly.
Breaking everything in their sight.
Leaving no mercy.
Taking down her heart too.
Leaving it like rotten fruit.

...

...

Dark and dirty.
With scratches and bruises.
Completely demolished.

Years went by.
She had all the time in the world to rebuild her safe zone.
But no strength was left.
Her will was gone.
Her power vanished.
So she waited.
For someone to come and help her recover from the pain and trauma.
But no one wants a broken doll.
A misused, beaten, little doll.

Alone she lived while years went by.
Without you, or them, or anyone, by her side.
Her tears dried up.
Her peachy fresh body turned to sharp edgy bones.
She no longer believed in Love.
And no longer cared about Life.
She just waited for it to all pass by.

And so it did.
Her only joy now is seeing her own ribs.
She doesn't let her cuts fade away.
She talks to no one -
Makes them all stay out of her way.

She is dying.
A slow painful death.
Look what you did to her.

Look what you did to me.

I am dying.

You are killing me.

Let me die. Let me go.

Where is the line between life and death?
And why can't we just cross it whenever we want?
Can a person be on the line?
Both dead and alive?
Or neither dead nor alive?
Why are we threatened with hell
when we simply want the pain to end?

Lost Control

—

Through the broken glass,
I can see the skeleton staring at me.
"Did you give up already?
You were never ready for this..."
She teases me, laughs in my face.
But it's okay,
My vision is blurry now,
Can hardly see through the tears that filled my swollen eyes.

"What have you done?"
The scream comes from nearby,
Yet feels like it is miles away.
Am I drowning?
No.
I'm sitting on my bedroom floor.
And still, everything seems distant.
My lungs are full.
I can not breathe.

The broken glass looked tempting.
I did what I thought was right.
But there's no time to reassure myself.
More screams, more worries.
The skeleton is still across from me.
I'm giving in.
You won.

Man in Black

—

With shampoo in my hair
And shower gel running down my back,
I hear an unexpected knock,
And realize that you came back,
Fully dressed in Black.

I run down as you scream for me,
And see you standing with your eyes inside of me.
"The Man in Black", they call you,
"The one that ends it all", they say.

I can't believe you came again to see me doing fine and well.
I told you not to come again,
I told you I was fine,
And yet you know me better than all,
Cause it is you that I desire.

...

...

So I welcome you
Back into my open arms,
As we sit and drink while remembering all the past
In which we could have been.
Until I left you for myself.

When I look up I see you staring.
This time not at me,
But right through me,
And that's when it hits me...

You have taken what was left of me,
As your lust for me could not be tamed.

Purple could have been the warmest color

I have read many books about military veterans
How they get war flashbacks
Stuck in a loop of PTSD
Consuming them

I too have PTSD
Flashbacks, but not of war
Of things You did to me, over and over again
And it's consuming me... and I will fight it no more

Purple could have been the warmest color

In the Eyes of an Ocean

—

Wave after Wave.

The visitors can't help coming by.
Smiles and laughter fill the night sky,
Exchanged looks of strangers,
Games played nearby.

Lonely teens and broken lovers,
Gazing up at the dreamy sky.
Hand in hand, the married couple,
Walking by, they can't say goodbye.

All alone the misplaced doll,
Waiting for time to burn.
Shattered, beaten, and misused,
Left alone completely bruised.

Let me help,
Let me take the pain away.
Let your breath escape from you,
And lose yourself in me today.

Taking her away,
I save her from herself,
Time does not heal,
But waves will help your soul stay sane.

Wave after Wave.

Freedom Wave

"You must purify yourself"
He hands me the blade and slowly steps away.
Waiting for the wave of sins to flood the unholy ground.
Counting seconds, he keeps his gaze on me,
Lost in the cruelty of this world that destroyed his love.
He blames me.
For all the wrong doing. For the misery he suffered.
And not for a moment does he realize his faults.
Denying the truth, he is convinced of my crime.
Lacking patience he takes the blade back and does destiny's work.

Covered in a pool of my own blood, he uses his hands
to carry me out.
For a moment, I am filled with hope that he will save me, find help.
So naïve.
With slow steps he reaches the cliff, and without a word,
tosses me Away into the open ocean, where I find myself
gasping for air.

My lungs refuse to operate,
I am disappearing into the darkness
with the blood red ocean ahead,
But greet the ocean floor kindly, as it takes me in with pride.
At last, I allow my eyelids to drop shut, finally feeling free.

I played hangman by myself last night

My thighs and wrists were painted red
but the paint would not stop dripping
So I drank medicine for my head
but it still would not stop spinning
That's when I made myself a choker necklace
but it was way too loose around my neck.

Some little girls should not be left alone...

Distortion

—

Her mind is playing tricks again.
This "imagination" seems too real.

Tick-Tock
He can't possibly be here.
Claws scraping on the wooden door,
Silent laughter, threatening grin.
Whispering "I am finally here".
Step by step, approaching her night-bed.
There is no need for that.
He took what he needed, her ability to Breathe.
Tick-Tock

She is suffocating.
Unable to let out a sound.
Choking on tears.
Fighting for her life.
Too late...
Her hands are tied,
Her eyes are shut.
A mute...

Day and Night won't pass without him stopping by.
She asks for help, they stare and laugh.
But they don't know she's just his start.

Distortion of the mind? Or is this life?
It is for You, dear reader, to decide.

i wish it would rain
—

the intoxicating warmth
of this hot November day
makes her long sleeve
sweater stick to her arms.

she tries to peel it off, but
her raw scars already sting, so
she tries to hide her discomfort in
hopes that no one notices.

next time she will be more careful and
slice her thighs instead with little
zebra cuts. or maybe she will
carve a word instead

and maybe the word will be 'help'
and maybe the word will be 'gone'

Surviving

...

I'm sorry Mama

—

My Mama always told me that I should never, ever, cry.
That I could only shed a tear, when someone very special died.

I kept that promise, Mama, for many, many, years.
But tonight, I'm filled with sorrow.
A river path has already been created from my eyes to my cheeks.
My body is shaking, My eyes are swollen, My jaw is clenched tight.
For I have lost someone very, very special to me.
Maybe no one can see, and maybe no one can tell, but, Mama,
I lost a little girl.

She ran from me far, far away.
Into the dark, deep, scary woods, where there was no way out.
I tried to help her, I tried to call out her name.
But she thought she could get out by herself. And told me not to help.
Oh Mama! You wouldn't believe what happened next!
He came behind her and slaughtered the little girl.
Mutilated her.
Until there was nothing left but blood and bones.

Oh Mama! I'm so sorry!
I'm sorry I could not get her out!
I'm sorry that I didn't try harder to help her escape!
Oh Mama! I'm sorry, I'm sorry!

The little, happy girl is gone.
But her killer is still on the loose.
He is swimming in glory and victory.
Showing off her stolen innocence as his award.

Oh Mama,
I'm sorry.
I'm sorry that she is gone.

Learning to breathe without you

—

Living without you is like living in a world with no oxygen

I'm suffocating
without you. My
insides hurt so much, it starts
to show on the
outside. I can no longer hide the
pain you've caused
when with me and the even greater
pain you caused when you left

Where do I search for you?
Where do I find you?

How do I breathe without you?

Healing

—

I spent years of my life waiting for someone to
love me
care for me
respect me
...

But no one did.

That is when I learned the power of
Self-love
Self-care
Self-respect

finding a four-leaf clover

—

After 2 years 5 months and 6 days
She left him
"Go have some fun"
He had all the fun with her
"Do what you love"
She was the only one he loved
"Find yourself!"
He already did
He found himself in her laugh
In her soft palms and smooth hands
In her wrinkles right by her eyes
In her mole on her left shoulder
In her scar above the belly button
In her toes that were always painted black
In her hair that smelled of daisies
He found himself in her worst fears
In her pet peeves
In her favorite books
In her daydreams
In her habits and in her confidence
In her

...

...

He found himself,
Or better yet,
His better self
When he was surrounded by her
So why did she do it?
Why did she leave?
It was to torture him
No
It was because she could not get used to his silly hair
No
It was because she never loved him
No
She did.
She loved him.
But that was not enough for her.

She wanted to love herself.

The Illusion of Freedom is My Biggest Dream.

—

How long until I can live my life outside my mind?

Reality is slipping away as I bury my face
into a black mirror that I use to escape.
And how I wish I could escape.
Live without the fear of a bleak future, by painting
my days with a rainbow of colors. Yet, I am surrounded by walls
built up by "loved" ones, who try
to protect me but are simply limiting me.
It cannot go on like this.
I long for freedom.
I shall set myself
Free

Where did you go
while I was sleeping?
—

In my dreams
I see you vividly, as you follow me around.
I see your puffy lips, your small blue eyes, you brown hair
that I could swear was dirty blonde,
I see your bushy eyebrows, your straight nose, your imperfect skin.
In my dreams, I see you.

As I open my eyes
You disappear without a trace, and although I know
Your features, and I know them well. I can't place them all
together.
Your face becomes the face of a stranger.
As I open my eyes, you cease to exist.

WOMAN

—

woman
The word rolls off your tongue like an insult.
You look down upon me,
Judge me for my desire to grow wings.
Your gaze is that of disgust and yet you draw me closer
With your filthy paws.

Woman
Is the one who gave you life.
And you dare to belittle her with your filthy mouth?
Why don't you compare her to the earth instead?
The ground that gives us food
Why don't you compare her to the air?
That lets us breathe
Why don't you compare her to water?
That can quench our thirst
Why don't you compare her to fire?
That keeps us warm

WOMAN
Is what I am
Is what I am proud to be
So don't touch me if I don't want to be touched
And don't stop me if I don't want to be stopped
But most importantly,
Don't feel pity for me because I was born a woman.
I can do what I please to do
And I will do it when I please to do it.
I am unstoppable.
I am a woman.

Change the things that makes you sad

I take off my skin
As if it is old, dirty clothes
That you damaged with your hands

I need to change

Reality

...

Why did you give in to the sweet temptation of death?
My mind yearns for it, as my heart yearns for you.
Although I no longer pray, you are always in
my prayers. But I would rather be with
you, wherever you are. And perhaps
if I too, give in, I will find
you.

Find Myself In You

You are always on my mind,
and I want you, I want you, I want you.

I said I wouldn't, but I lied. I
Will open the window for you if you
Promise to visit me once more. I
Will let you enter and stay with me tonight, if you
Promise not to leave me again.
Not even if I ask.
Not even if I beg.

Even strangers think of you

—

I wonder if all poets write about you.
A version of you
that I will never know
or never see
or never want to be with.
Endless poems filled with your thoughts and actions and feelings

What I'd do to bring
you back into my arms:

I will dance with you
when your energy surpasses that of the
sun, but won't that be easy for you?

I will sin more, because I know
I won't find you in heaven.
I will read more, to
feed my imagination of us together.
I will only whisper, so you are
forced to lean in and listen to my words.
I will become your sugar, your alcohol, your cigarettes, your drugs
I will become anything to make you stay...

To be with you, or not to be at all
—

If I could choose to be reborn as anything I wanted, I would
choose the sunset, in hopes that you would finally
look at me.
Perhaps, I would choose the rain, with the intention of feeling
your skin. Or else, I would choose
the strongest ocean wave, so I could pull
you deep down and keep you
to myself

Deal with the Devil

—

Is it a sin to remember you five years too late?
To think of your soft lips and rough hands?
To wish that you would come back?

The more I think, the more I realize that I don't mind
sinning. I will make a deal with the devil, and sacrifice
all I've got. I will bathe in blood under the full moon, and lay
in a circle of crystals. I will do anything and everything.

Just please,
come back.

Unwanted

—

At 22:00, I started drinking to ease the pain away, to
calm down, to let loose.
drink after drink after drink
Glasses are being refilled without my asking. A magic trick.
At 00:00, I can no longer stand but I still think straight, I
know I haven't reached my limit yet. There's
still a goal to reach, a purpose to serve.
I drink I drink I drink
No longer knowing which glass is mine, I take a large gulp.
At 02:00, you are on my mind. Your face blurry,
a man unknown to me.
Your faults are long forgotten. The ringing in my ear is replaced
with your whisper, and
I want you I want you I want you

Come lay with me?

If I summon you like a demon
will you stay the night?

Is that all there is to life?

—

Is that all there is to life?

She dreads going to sleep,
for she knows, she will wake
up to see tomorrow.
She fills her stomach up with
Red Bull and Modafinil,
praying that one of them
will keep her eyes from
closing shut. But she knows.
She knows that no matter
how much she tries to
stretch out this wretched day,
tomorrow will come.
And she will live on.
Because she was too afraid to make it stop.

Is that all there is to life?

G r o u n d h o g

D a y

Scrolling through your feed
over and over
again. Until my eyes are too
tired to focus on your face. Until my
mind starts imagining you by my side. Until my
skin feels your lips on me. Again.

Will I ever find out if death is as peaceful as it sounds?

Maybe tomorrow

scrolling my life away

—

i wish i could put my thoughts on paper,
my imagination on a canvas

i wish i could capture my greatest fears and
my deepest desires

but i am no artist.

my thoughts will stay hidden and my needs
unfulfilled

i will be carried away by the tide, and
blown away by the wind

until nothing remains.

Searching for Nirvana

—

Play the music loud enough to
drown my thoughts, until
all I hear is the silence ringing in my mind

At 1 am, I want you.

—

At 2am

I get a sudden urge to call you, to hear your voice.
Your absence let itself be known and I worry that I'm
missing you too much. When I don't want to even think about you.
Banishing you from my thoughts has done no
wonders. When you still show up in my dreams.

At 3am

I have lost to myself.
I have called you.
But the kind female voice has informed me that your number
is no longer valid. And I don't know
if I feel relieved that you are no longer there
to rely on, or worried. For your number was my
prayer. That I would repeat to hush my worries away.

At 4am

I realize that your absence has left
emptiness that I will never replace.
I have already tried with all the possible options, and everything
failed. Over and over and over again. And yet I still crave you
like a child, who knows no better,
craves sweets that will cause more harm than good. But
my health can't deteriorate much longer.
I won't survive till sunrise.
Maybe I should give in and finally accept this
emptiness as a part of me.
Allow it to live within me.
Give into the fear of utter consumption and loneliness.

let me go

—

Here I am, once again,
trying to wash away my sins,
unable to get rid of the imprint on my soul

My memory of you is a pixelated image, the
resolution keeps getting worse with every
passing year.

Fading Away

Will Fate lead me back to you?

—

If the red string of fate is tied to you, I will
chop my fingers off to set myself free.

Do you still remember me?

—

        I can't think bad of you and that is why I
                        hate myself
    Who do you think of on the nights you want to be loved?

When I opened the window for you
You let the summer heat come in
But I didn't mind
I traded it for your warm kiss

to love or not to love

Crying till I go blind

—

The memory of you is fading
But I want to cling onto your skin
I want to look into your ice cold eyes
That at times resembled the color of the ocean
But lacked all it's depth
So beautiful yet so empty

Infesting my Soul

—

I wish I could kill all these thoughts of you
That are crawling into my mind like
tiny little spiders

Prayers left unheard

—

I'm on my knees
Asking you to take me to you
But God, like always,
Answers me with silence

Changing with the Seasons

—

It often feels like all my problems can
be pinpointed to you
Like a map where all the roads
lead to one location
Despair, Guilt, and Anger
All of it because of you.
But that's not exactly true,
Is it?

If I die while gasping for air
the scent I will last
inhale will be of your
cologne.
You can choke me however hard you want
I will only feel the
softness of your firm hands
Considering myself
blessed with every bit of your
touch.

Such a lovely way to die

No longer beside me

—

When it gets cold at night, and I
reach for your hand,
Why do I get surprised when I
grab the blanket instead?

310899

—

Feeling God's presence disappearing,
day by day.
I stay up at night
not recognizing who I have become.
Washing away my sins with water,
not fearing the wrath of the almighty,
like I felt the wrath of the woman that birthed me
when she found out about you.
But on this day, I still think about you...
I still love you...

Let me go.
Or else I will turn into the
water you hold tightly in your palms and
drip away so slowly, that you won't

notice my presence disappearing from your

life.

But slowly, yet surely,

I will let myself go.

Drip away like water

see me as a different person

—

My vision blurs as I stand up, my
lack of vitamins is showing. But maybe
what I lack is you.
The disappearing sight is a
blessing, for I no longer see my sins.

good for nothing but art

—

"all these artists write about love,
but i will be different"
a constant lie we tell ourselves,
not realizing that everything in this world
brings us back to
love.
all the things we do,
all the things that make life worth living,
brings us back to
love.

to cut is to sculpture. i am art.

I cut with the hope of killing the
parts of me that I cannot control. The
parts of me that I hate.
The cut is deep, but not deep enough to
kill these parts. To
kill these thoughts that are eating me alive.

losing myself

when did my thoughts turn into the words you've
chanted into my ears? when did my mind become a
mirror of yours?

whisper slowly into my ear

—

I refuse to look at the
wonders of the world. My eyes were only
meant for you. After all these years they are
decaying with the beauty of
your soul, that I will
never love again. With every growing
temptation to gain a glimpse of what
I'm missing, I search for you
in all of my dreams. For you to know I
won't cheat, I gouge my eyes out with
my claws that I sharpened to protect myself
from you. And here I cave to the sound of
your voice

If you can hear me, give me a sign...

—

On days like these
When I'm bawling on the floor
Thoughts of my hidden razor slipping into my mind
I beg god to give me the strength to live on
Wondering how things have gone so wrong
But a slight cut wouldn't kill. It would let me feel the
pain I deserve.
So maybe just one. A little one. In a secret place where
no one will see it and
no one will know.
Or perhaps a bruise?
How will they know it was self-induced?
God. Please, God. Help me.

Who needs air,

I wanted you to need me
Like a man needs air
But you needed me
Like a smoker needs a cig
I should be furious,
But on days like these,
I wish you needed me,
Once more.

when I can have you instead?

I will see you soon. I promise.

—

I mourn for your soul,
two years too late, with tears that I promised you
would fill a river. We talked about death but I prayed
I'd be the first to go. So why is life so cruel?
Why did it let death take you away
when you were promised to me?

If the future is without you, I don't want to live through it.

Future plans, future dreams, future thoughts
All had one thing in common
You
No matter where I saw myself, it was always with you.
I am now living in the future, but you haven't made it through.
Forever in the past.

Unattainable Life

—

I'm only alone with you
In my mind,
Unattainable joy
That I will die for,
To be with you
I will live in your skin,
Like a blanket over my soul,
Finally, feel your love.
Life with you
Is a house on fire
And I love feeling the warmth
Radiating from your hands.

Keeper of Memories

—

What happens now?
All our shared moments turned into memories, but have these
memories died with you? Am I the only one that possesses
and stores these special moments? How could you
leave me with such an important task? How will I
preserve you in these memories?
How do I make you stay?

Mourn for You

—

If I visit her dressed in black
with flowers in my hands, will she see my sad eyes
past the smile? Will she know that
I mourn for her son? Will she see that
I mourned for him all these years?
Will she let me in?
Will she give me the right
to keep mourning?

Acknowledgements

...

All these poems are for you.
I was for you.

You died in 2020.
Back when we met, I was 15 and you were 17.
Now I'm 21, the same age you will remain forever.
Rest in peace my love. I hope to see you soon.

I regret not contacting you sooner.
I'm sorry I took so long. I'm sorry I was too late.
I'm sorry that I wasn't there for you
like you were there for me all those years ago.
I'm sorry, Chris.

Redaction

Redaction is a bespoke typeface commissioned by
Titus Kaphar and Reginald Dwayne Betts' for their
Redaction exhibition at MoMA PS1. It was designed by
Jeremy Mickel and Forest Young and as part of the
artists' dedication to social justice and legal
equity, is distributed under the Open Font License.

JetBrains Mono

JetBrains Mono is a monospace typeface designed by
Philipp Nurullin and Konstantin Bulenkov at
JetBrains, to be used in the company's developer
products. It is licensed under the Open Font License
in its spirit of being a tool for programmers that
can be maintained by the community.

Thank You

Huge thank you to my two great friends, Kartik and
Karim, for helping me with the fonts and layout.
This poetry compilation would have taken an even
longer time to be completed without your support.
I hope that everyone out there has friends as good
as you guys are to me.

<3

www.ingramcontent.com/pod-product-compliance
Lightning Source LLC
Chambersburg PA
CBHW071200130726
47998CB00002B/558